BUSINESS
SELLING
INSIGHTS
VOL. 3

BUSINESS SELLING INSIGHTS

VOL. 3

SPOTLIGHTS ON LEADING BUSINESS INTERMEDIARIES, BROKERS, AND M&A ADVISORS

FEATURING LEADING BUSINESS INTERMEDIARIES, BROKERS, AND M&A ADVISORS

Douglas Brown

Dale Armor

Jackie Ossin Hirsch

Jason Hullender

Joshua Carnes

Robert Latham

Ben Hargis

Kate Vriner

Gerry Chadwick

Ed Sadler

Business Selling Insights Vol. 3/ Mark Imperial —1st ed.
Managing Editor/ Shannon Buritz

ISBN: 978-1-954757-20-2

Remarkable Press™

Royalties from the retail sales of **"BUSINESS SELLING INSIGHTS Vol 3: SPOTLIGHTS ON LEADING BUSINESS INTERMEDIARIES, BROKERS, AND M&A ADVISORS"** are donated to the Global Autism Project:

The Global Autism Project 501(C)3 is a nonprofit organization that provides training to local individuals in evidence-based practice for individuals with autism.

The Global Autism Project believes that every child has the ability to learn, and their potential should not be limited by geographical bounds.

The Global Autism Project seeks to eliminate the disparity in service provision seen around the world by providing high-quality training to individuals providing services in their local community. This training is made sustainable through regular training trips and contiguous remote training.

You can learn more about the Global Autism Project and make direct donations by visiting **GlobalAutismProject.org.**

CONTENTS

A NOTE TO THE READER

Thank you for obtaining your copy of "BUSINESS SELLING INSIGHTS Vol. 3: Spotlights on Leading Business Intermediaries, Brokers, and M&A Advisors." This book was originally created as a series of live interviews on my business podcast; that's why it reads like a series of conversations, rather than a traditional book that talks at you.

My team and I have personally invited these professionals to share their knowledge because they have demonstrated that they are true advocates for the success of their clients and have shown their great ability to educate the public on the topic of buying and selling businesses.

I wanted you to feel as though the participants and I are talking with you, much like a close friend or relative, and felt that creating the material this way would make it easier for you to grasp the topics and put them to use quickly, rather than wading through hundreds of pages.

So relax, grab a pen and paper, take notes, and get ready to learn some fascinating insights from our Leading Business Intermediaries, Brokers, and M&A Advisors.

Warmest regards,

Mark Imperial

Publisher, Author, and Radio Personality

INTRODUCTION

"BUSINESS SELLING INSIGHTS Vol. 3: Spotlights on Leading Business Intermediaries, Brokers, and M&A Advisors" is a collaborative book series featuring leading professionals from across the country.

Remarkable Press™ would like to extend a heartfelt thank you to all participants who took the time to submit their chapter and offer their support in becoming ambassadors for this project.

100% of the royalties from this book's retail sales will be donated to the Global Autism Project. Should you want to make a direct donation, visit their website at **GlobalAutismProject.org**

DOUGLAS BROWN

CONVERSATION WITH DOUGLAS BROWN

■ **Douglas, you are the founder of TheBusinessDealer.com in Williamsburg, Virginia. Tell us about your work and the people you help.**

Douglas Brown: I am a business broker and advisor, and my clients are typically Main Street businesses, small businesses with $5 million a year revenue or less. I don't specialize in a particular type of business within that space because, although each business sector is a bit different in the details, the issues and processes for selling a small business are all pretty much the same. It gets different in the valuation and in the sets of buyers who may be interested in that type of business.

I do my business brokerage with Transworld. Among other advantages, Transworld gives me access to the tools for a comprehensive valuation within a sector. In addition to those expensive database services, we also see hundreds of our own listings, which gives us a good sense of what businesses are selling for right now.

The other way we lend value to a seller is the ability to find buyers. Transworld is a national company with hundreds of brokers nationwide and thousands of listings, and we sell more listings than any other broker network. Somebody who doesn't buy one listing will often shift their attention to another. That gives us regular interactions with a larger pool of potential buyers, and we have people with experience selling almost any kind of business you can imagine. If you can get a business license for it, we've probably sold one somewhere!

■ How prepared and informed are business owners when it comes time to sell?

Douglas Brown: Not many sellers have sold a business before! A few serial business owners buy one, sell one, and then buy another. For most sellers, it is a significant milestone in a small business owner's life, and it is one they only come across once. It's also one they are not usually well-prepared to handle.

Obviously, when I first meet a business owner, I will not try to get them to sell their business right away! There is a time and place when that will be the right thing to do. In fact, the trouble begins when someone calls me and says, "I need to sell right away."

For most business owners, exit planning needs to happen right away. Most people think, "I am not planning to exit right away, so I will get to it someday." My experience with most sellers is that Dame Fortune has a habit of playing tricks on us and that "someday" ends up being tomorrow. Perhaps you get sick, have a family issue, your business becomes uninteresting to you, or you have a great opportunity elsewhere. And all of a sudden, you want to sell.

Often when I get those panic calls, it is from an owner who has tried to sell their business themselves. Or I get in a conversation with an owner who wants to do that to save on the commission. So let me set that straight. You've never done it before. It's your most significant single investment other than maybe your home (for most people, even more than their home), and you want to learn by "doing?" For something you're only ever going to do once? That is a really bad plan, and I can tell you that from personal experience selling my own business!

■ Are there myths and misconceptions about selling a business?

Douglas Brown: The most challenging part of my job is setting realistic expectations with a seller. Many of them have seen too many Wall Street movies, seen and heard about dot-coms, and so on. And many of them think that they're going to retire on the proceeds of their small business. Some of them will. But the hard truth is that it's not going to work that way for a significant number of them. I would love it, of course, because we're paid on commission if we could sell every business in the multimillion-dollar range. But the reality is that many small business owners have worked on their business for 10 to 15 years, and it's only going to fetch them a few hundred thousand dollars when they sell, or maybe only a couple. That's certainly not enough to retire on. So the biggest myth is that "I worked all these years to build something up, and now I'm going to use it to retire on." It's just not that way.

■ What common mistakes do sellers make?

Douglas Brown: Aside from thinking they will do a good job of trying to sell it themselves, which we already mentioned, the biggest mistake that a seller can make as we're having a conversation is to be untruthful. And I don't mean that they're puffing the value of their business because we expect that. We expect to hear things like, "These are the highest quality donuts in town." But I can't help them sell if they are not fully honest and transparent with me about what is going on with the business.

Many of the things they can do to make it easier to sell are all tied together. For example, if you can't produce decent numbers on your business, selling will be tough because that is the first thing the buyer wants to see. The harder it is for the buyer to get decent information about the business, the more they will be skeptical about what it is they're being offered. So number one is, "Don't lie to me." Many buyers don't want to tell me they are not making any money - actually, I think what is really going on is they don't want to admit it to themselves. But we're going to find that out as soon as we see the tax returns. Now, I can take their "say so" numbers and try to market the business. But the big problem with that is as soon as the buyer starts looking at it and doing their due diligence, if things aren't reasonably aligned with what they were told, they will just walk away. They're not going to spend three weeks trying to figure out what's going on with your numbers and what the real numbers are in your business, and they're not going to invest $100 or more per hour for their CPA to try and unravel it for you. Instead, they're going to assume that every rock they pick up has another scorpion under it, and they're just going to walk away. So, be honest, truthful, and realistic about what is possible.

I understand that we all want to sell our businesses for as much as possible, and I would love to help all my clients reach the price of their dreams. All I can do is help you sell for as much as is really possible. Unfortunately, the buyers have access to the same kind of buyer business websites that the sellers also looked at, creating a range of expected values. That's your reality. Now, your particular business, for reasons that we can help portray in the selling process, may be worth more than other businesses like it. But if most businesses in that niche are selling for, let's say, three times the net value, and you offer for eight times the net value, buyers are simply not going to bother looking at it at all. They will say, "I'm not even going to talk to the seller because they're divorced from reality. So I can't trust anything they tell me, and I'm not going to waste my time with them." You can't explain yourself or negotiate with them unless you can get them looking at your business in the first place. So part of the game is to get the asking price into a zone that the seller will believe. They will then be interested in getting the additional disclosure material to explain why they should pay more for this business than the three other ones like it for sale.

■ Is it a good time to sell a business in today's market?

Douglas Brown: Yes, it is. In general. It's a tough time to sell a business if you're a high-labor, high customer-service business because effects are still lingering in some states where the customers, the employees, or the governor are still acting the way they did when we didn't know anything about COVID. If your revenues and profits fell off the table in 2020 and are still not back to where they were in 2019, it won't be easy to get a fair price.

Most impacted, probably, are restaurants. Bless their hearts; I love those restaurant guys. What would life be like without them? And if you're running a good restaurant, you can make a lot of money. But there are a lot of restaurants that are kind of marginal, and it's a grinding business even in the best of times. The owners are tired of putting in the hours, but they can't bear the idea of selling it for $50,000 to $100,000. They think that at least their equipment must be worth some portion of all of the money someone would have to spend to buy it all and install it. But, no, it's not, at least not in 2022. Your equipment is worth nothing because hundreds of thousands of restaurants around the country went out of business in 2020, 2021, and still in 2022. The owner got tired of shoveling money into a lease or payroll for an empty or even closed restaurant, walked away from the lease, and left the equipment. And if you want to start a restaurant with nothing down, I can fix you up in Virginia, and any commercial real estate agent can help you in any other state. You can just go find the space and agree to lease it. There will probably be a complete setup there for you. So for small, under-performing restaurants that don't own the real estate, yes, it's brutal.

For most other businesses, there are two huge factors at work to make it a good time to sell (or to buy, for that matter): market instability and continued government funding.

While the market runup of 2018 to 2021 has been great for investors, what goes up will at some point go down. Investors with money will want to diversify. A well-run and well-established small business should throw off 15 to 25 percent net revenue on a consistent basis (larger businesses are satisfied to earn much less because they have a corporate staff on overhead). If it doesn't, it is probably taking on discretionary expenses, which also flow back to the owner. Most of them provide essential services to a local market, and the need for them doesn't change with national economic trends. If you're looking at a hedge against volatility, you can't do much better than a proven small business.

The second big factor at work in 2022 is that the government hasn't finished with the small business programs created during COVID. A lot of the money is still out there, seeking only to be used in viable deals at ridiculously low interest. When money is readily available at a low cost, people will spend it more readily, pushing higher deal prices.

If there's a viable business out there, people are looking to buy it. And it's a great time to sell even if other businesses are also selling because that tells a buyer that making money in that sector isn't a fluke. When many businesses can prosper in a niche, buyers can feel more comfortable that they too have a reasonable chance to make money.

Let's address one of the other myths. People say, "Small businesses are very risky." You see all of these numbers about 80% of small businesses failing every year. But those are startups, not proven businesses. Find a small business that's been in operation for three or four years, regularly turning a profit. If you buy it and just keep doing what it is doing, you should be able to earn the same level of profit. If you want to grow it, you will have to change something, and that's the risk-reward dynamic. You profit if it works, and it's on you if you end up breaking it. So small businesses are actually very stable and reliable investments. As a seller, if you can show that your business operates reliably and turns a dependable profit, you'll find buyers.

■ **Douglas, what inspired you to get started in this field?**

Douglas Brown: The truth is I got into this field about 15 years too late! I did have a small business at one time, and it was doing pretty well. And then I got told my Reserve unit was being activated for the Gulf War. I didn't want my business calling me from 10,000 miles away, wanting another few thousand bucks to cover payroll or something, so I went ahead with selling it. I didn't know at the time that business brokers even existed. I did sell it at a reasonable price, and that's where the problems began. Twenty years later, the litigation to get it all paid is still underway!

After all that transpired, I was doing business consulting for a couple of decades. During that time, Transworld contacted me and said, "Look, you're doing all this business value consulting. Have you thought about business brokering?" I didn't even know this was a thing, but I looked into it, and it clicked for me immediately. Now, I enjoy meeting with business owners and talking about their business situation, helping them portray their business in a way that people can understand. I help them work through the difficulties as well, like, "Hey, maybe this baby is a little uglier than you think. But we can still do something with it." So it's great. I just love it, and it's a wonderful business.

■ How can people find you, connect with you, and learn more?

Douglas Brown: You can find me on my website at www.the busi-nessdealer.com. I've provided some comprehensive free resources for both buyers and sellers, and you can make an appointment right from that site. I'll be happy to assist you in making an exit plan, selling a business, or buying one. I work with Transworld Business Advisors, and I have a site there also https://www.tworld.com/agent/douglasbrown/. We have thousands of listings, and they're ready for you right now if you're planning on buying.

The general advice in this chapter applies to most businesses in most jurisdictions. As of 2022, 17 of the 50 states require that only a real estate professional licensed in that state may advise you on buying or selling a specific business in that state. Douglas Brown is licensed to conduct real estate transactions in the Commonwealth of Virginia.

DOUGLAS BROWN, PH.D.

Founder

TheBusinessDealer.com

After serving as an Army officer, Douglas has spent his professional career as a business advisor helping organizations forecast and control their finances and implement effective management practices. With a growing focus on value delivery, it was a natural transition to business brokerage - what better definition of value than how much someone would pay for the business? With many years in the Washington DC metropolitan area, he has particular expertise with that area's unique businesses as well as the "normal" Main Street businesses found in the Virginia Peninsula, where he is now based. Douglas is a licensed real estate salesperson in Virginia and, as such, is permitted to assist clients in buying or selling businesses that have real estate attached. Douglas regrets to report that he is a total nerd and loves building business models on spreadsheets. Otherwise, he and his family enjoy the many offerings of the Williamsburg area, usually accompanied by the family dog.

EMAIL:
douglas.brown@thebusinessdealer.com

PHONE:
202-314-5199

WEBSITE:
https://thebusinessdealer.com

LINKEDIN:
www.linkedin.com/in/douglasbrownpm

FACEBOOK:
https://www.facebook.com/TheBusinessDealer

DALE
ARMOR

CONVERSATION WITH DALE ARMOR

> ■ **Dale, you are the Owner of Acquisition Experts, LLC in South Florida. Tell us about your work and the people you help.**

Dale Armor: I've been a business intermediary full-time for 27 years here in South Florida. South Florida is very global and transient, so the buyers come from all over the world. As far as sellers, we service the east coast of South Florida, from Orlando down through the Florida Keys. We typically represent 80 to 100 companies for sale at any given time. We are a licensed Florida real estate corporation. We list businesses for sale on a contract to procure a buyer, similar to how a residential realtor lists a house. We are members of the Business Brokers of Florida, a cooperating multi-list service (MLS) of participating and qualified Florida business brokerage firms. We love meeting the sellers, hearing their stories and backgrounds, how they got to where they are, and understanding what they are trying to accomplish. I'm intrigued by the study of varying business models. How they make money and what assets, inventory, and obligations are involved in the process is very interesting work. Once we have assisted the seller in preparing the company for a confidential sale, we market the business and find their best suitor. Buyers come from all over the globe, including the Northeast, Midwest, California, Canada, Europe, South Africa, and South America. It's fascinating work.

■ Have you seen more buyers due to the "Great Resignation?"

Dale Armor: Absolutely. Florida is a gold rush right now; people are moving here in droves. They say about 1,000 people a day are moving to Florida, and it's really not a great employment market, necessarily. So, buying a job or buying a small business is a great alternative. No one can fire you, lay you off, or tell you what to do. It's your business. On the sell side, many owners wanted to sell ten years ago or more and missed the window due to the last recession of 2008. Many of our sellers are older and held the business longer than they wanted to while the economy recovered. They don't want to miss out on selling now before inflation, rising interest rates, or other global affairs affect the value of their business enterprise.

■ Are there myths and misconceptions regarding selling a business?

Dale Armor: There is a lack of education regarding planning an exit strategy in advance. We work with CPAs and wealth managers to form relationships with their clients three to five years before they would like to exit and sell the business. We create an exit strategy to clean up their books and records, streamline operations and reduce the business's dependence on the owner to maximize profitability and make the business financeable through an SBA small business loan. Many people come to us wanting to sell their business, not giving the appropriate consideration as to how valuable their business enterprise is to their overall net worth at retirement. As a result, their books and records aren't clean, they don't report all the sales, and they have other value detractors limiting the resale value of their business. The problem is you can't have your cake and eat it too, so to speak. The books and records have to be clean to maximize the sale price. A big part of my job is providing education to business owners to assist them in preparing their company for sale.

■ How far ahead should owners prepare when thinking about selling their business?

Dale Armor: For a business to be financeable through an SBA loan where a qualified buyer could come in with 10% to 20% down, and the seller gets cashed out and doesn't have to be the bank, the seller needs to have two to three years of supporting tax returns that show the historical cash flow of the business can service the debt the buyer is going to incur to buy the business, pay that buyer a salary, and have a cushion in the cash flow of approximately 25%. This is referred to as a 1.25% debt service coverage ratio. It's imperative the seller starts strategically planning their exit strategy approximately five years out by speaking with a qualified business intermediary and their accountant to create a game plan. The final three years before they sell, they need well-documented earnings to maximize the price and make the business financeable.

■ What mistakes do you help sellers avoid?

Dale Armor: There are several, so we'll touch on a couple. The most important thing we want to help a seller avoid is sabotaging the business value by intentionally driving down the profits of the business. When selling a business, cash flow is king. The seller must have strong EBITDA right on their corporate tax returns' face page. Unfortunately, throughout the year and more typically towards the end of the year, it is common for small business owners to realize they will pay significant taxes. They naturally want to minimize their tax liability. At this juncture, they may make major expenditures, not deposit cash, bury personal expenses in the business or decide they won't deposit certain business income such as Accounts Receivable until the following year. They are trying to drive the business's profit down to minimize tax consequences, but that is the wrong strategy to maximize the sale of the business. A qualified business intermediary can recast or normalize the seller's discretionary earnings to show a buyer and a lender what the seller has historically made in total cash flow and benefits.

Another big mistake is many small businesses are entirely dependent on the seller or the seller's relationships. On larger sales, no one wants to buy a business that is completely wrapped around the owner.

■ Dale, what inspired you to get started in this field?

Dale Armor: Well, I got into it by accident in 1993, at the age of 33, with two children under five. My wife was a stockbroker at the time and opted to become a homemaker. I had a proverbial gun to my head to become successful and support my family. Fear motivation is a wonderful thing when you're in outside sales. My brother-in-law gave me great advice when he said, "Always work in the client's best interest. Don't think about the money. Only think about providing service, solving problems, and working in the best interest of the client." It was probably the best advice I ever received. Our agents always focus on the client and their goals. By being trusted advisors and helping other people get what they want, we ultimately get what we want, a successful closing of business sale that's a win/win for all involved parties.

■ **Do you have any words of advice for someone getting ready to sell their business?**

Dale Armor: Make a plan to consult with your wealth manager, CPA, and a qualified Business Intermediary that will all collectively work in your best interest. Speak to your spouse and make sure they are on board with the strategies being developed. Explore all of your options from a family succession plan, possible sale to a key employee or multiple employees, a sale to a strategic buyer, or a sale in the open market. We can help you ascertain your best options when it comes to selling.

■ **How can people find you, connect with you, and learn more?**

Dale Armor: You can Google Acquisition Experts or go directly to our website at www.acquisitionexperts.net. We're easy to find and would love to assist. We don't mind giving clients a free broker's Opinion of Value of what their business is worth. This is a very important place to start before deciding to sell. A seller needs to understand the value of their business and what factors are adding to the value or reciprocally detracting from the value. Many owners come to us and say, "Well, I want a million dollars for my business." We may have to advise them that they can't get that right now because of multiple factors affecting value. We can advise them that we could get them their million dollars if they execute A, B, C, and

D and come back to us in two years. Everything continually circles back to client education. We're always happy to provide that for our clients and the clients of our referral sources such as CPAs and wealth managers.

DALE ARMOR

M&A Advisor, V.P.

South Florida Business Brokers of Florida and
BBF State Board Member, Member IBBA

Acquisition Experts, LLC

Dale is an exceptionally experienced and accomplished Business
Intermediary, having closed over 250 business sales. His focus is
representing Sellers of lower middle market companies seeking

acquisition by Strategic Buyers as a platform, add-on, or margin contribution addition to their existing portfolios.

EMAIL:
dale@acquisitionexperts.net

PHONE:
772-220-4455

WEBSITE:
www.acquisitionexperts.net

LINKEDIN:
https://www.linkedin.com/in/dalearmor/

WEBSITE BIO:
https://acquisitionexperts.net/about-us/meet-the-experts/dale-armor/

OTHER:
https://www.bizbuysell.com/business-broker/dale-armor/acquisition-experts-llc/581/

JACKIE OSSIN HIRSCH

CONVERSATION WITH JACKIE OSSIN HIRSCH

■ **Jackie, you are the founder of Crowne Atlantic Business Brokers in Orlando, Florida. Tell us about your work and the people you help.**

Jackie Ossin Hirsch: We've been selling companies since 2004 here at Crowne Atlantic, and I've been selling companies since 1998. We help stable, cash-flowing, successful businesses sell to the right buyer. Companies specialize in all sorts of goods and services. But our buyers want consistent, stable cash flow with great books and records and a business they can take to the next level. Buyers are looking for a business with a solid foundation led by an entrepreneur looking to retire.

- ## What types of businesses and what size businesses do you primarily sell?

Jackie Ossin Hirsch: We typically sell businesses with an EBIT or Owner Benefit of $500,000 to $5,000,000 and gross sales from $1,000,000 to $20,000,000. We mainly sell manufacturing, online companies, construction companies, service businesses, large restaurants, chains of restaurants, and other unique businesses with and without real estate.

- ## What do you think sellers need to know that they don't find in books about selling a business?

Jackie Ossin Hirsch: Sellers need to know that selling a business is emotional, personal, and it can be a very stressful experience if the business isn't put on the market properly and if the broker doesn't communicate properly with the seller.

- ## What types of questions do you get from owners thinking about selling?

Jackie Ossin Hirsch: There's a lot of soul searching that business owners have to do. One of my first deals happened when I was 22, and the seller was 65. He actually started crying out of the blue, and I had to figure out what to do and say in this scenario. And this has happened many times since. A business is a creation they have made. They have controlled it even more than a child, in many ways, because they created it from nothing. And many of my entrepreneurs started with nothing. Their concerns have to do with the legacy of the business, how to transition properly, and how to deal with the mental and emotional strain of the process. They have tax questions. They have questions about where they need to be physically. There's a company that I sold recently, and the seller said, "I have this vacation that I planned. I leave March 15, and I'll be two days short on the training time with the new owner." I said, "Listen, we will get that okayed by the buyer. You need to go, and when you come back, we will call you, and everything will be fine." We need to have that conversation and make sure they really feel comfortable with the process. I talk to my sellers about financing and finding the right buyer. It's not just about selling a company; it's about making a match.

■ Are there myths and misconceptions about selling a business?

Jackie Ossin Hirsch: Yes. Once, during the process of selling a company, the seller said, "Well, my friend just sold his company, and it was ten times earnings." But his friend's company was also netting 5 million EBIT, while his company was netting $500,000 EBIT. Don't get me wrong, $500,000 EBIT is great, but it's going to be a very different sale. And it's going to be a different EBIT (earnings before interest and tax), which is typically how multiples are created.

Multiples change not only by industry but by size. So a multiple of something that's netting $100,000 versus something that's netting $10 million is entirely different.

I think it's important to understand how to value the business and what elements you need as an owner. I also think owners should take a step back and ask, "Would I pay that amount for my business?" Suppose a seller wants to list their business for $10 million. In that case, they need to ask themselves, "Would I pay $10 million for this business?" That really gets them thinking. Sometimes the answer is yes because they genuinely have something spectacular. But sometimes it is no, and they have to think about that. They need to look at it from a few different perspectives.

In addition, clean books and records make a huge difference. A lot of times, a seller will say, "Oh well, if they're in the business, they'll understand." No, they won't understand, and neither will the bank. So you need to show what the business is making and pay the taxes if you want to maximize the company's value.

■ How has the "Great Resignation" impacted your market?

Jackie Ossin Hirsch: That's a fascinating question. First of all, I'm in Florida. The market in Florida is very different from other states. There's a ton of people moving to Florida. And it has been that way for a long time. People come to escape cold temperatures, and many want to retire here. But retirement has changed dramatically. Retirement now might mean 'retiring from a job and buying a business.' We have buyers resigning from large corporations, evolving their life through buying a business to doing something they've always wanted to do. They want to do it here in Florida. Business inventory moves very quickly, and there's not a lot of it. We've always had a total surplus of buyers and a deficit of sellers. But now, even more so. And the multiples have increased significantly at this point.

> ■ **Speaking of multiples and EBIT, how does it happen that we see crazy meme stock news where corporations sell for 100 times revenue?**

Jackie Ossin Hirsch: Well, that's very interesting. Recently, an electric car company was valued higher than GM, which is hard to wrap my head around. But it's about stockholders and public participation. With a private business, you don't have those same types of multiples, and a bank has to make that cash flow. When you have a public company, you have all these people willing to give the company money when they buy stock, so they don't have the same type of cash flow constraints as far as repaying debt. They're essentially giving away equity. So it's a whole different structure. When we deal with small private businesses priced $20 million and under, it's just a whole different way of cash-flowing deals, and it's about turning cash. That's why the perspective is entirely different. You'll never see those enormous multiples unless it's some radical invention that's going to change the world. We're dealing with brick-and-mortar businesses and online businesses. You can almost look at the online companies as being very similar to brick and mortar businesses, even if they're drop shopped because the focus is on recurring revenue and cash flow. Our buyers are looking for cash flow, and it's almost like a dividend stock. Sometimes a dividend stock is valued differently than a stock that doesn't pay dividends because the non-dividend stock will have more cash to work with that they don't have to payout.

■ **What are your top 5 tips for sellers in preparing their business for sale?**

Jackie Ossin Hirsch:

1. Prepare the paperwork! Clean books and records are a must! Organization will be rewarded with a higher purchase price. Buyers rely on clear systematic financial systems to be in place.

2. Reward key employees to keep them in place! Companies with a full management team in place and an owner who works *on the business* rather than *in the business* are worth so much more.

3. Fine-tune systems and processes! Buyers want a company with systems and processes in place that can help propel the business to the next level.

4. Make your business look as physically attractive as possible.

5. Make the online presence of your business look as attractive as possible. Websites should be updated with no broken links or old pages. Positive Google reviews and reviews on other sites are definitely helpful. If your business has been featured in the news, that should be included in your website, with links to the original article/video.

■ Jackie, what inspired you to get started in this field?

Jackie Ossin Hirsch: Sometimes, when you're 22, and you do something, you don't realize how hard it is. You think everything is hard because it's all new to you, so you just do it. But for me, I've always loved business. I've had several businesses that I've started and sold or started and grown. I invest in other people's businesses through SAFEs, convertible notes, series A rounds, dividend investments, and equity purchases, and it's fun for me. And I relate to the other business owners because I started with nothing, just like most business owners. I didn't use loans, and I didn't have family money, and I just really wanted to grow something.

I've been interested in business since I was a kid. One of my friends always mentions that when I was in school, the teacher once asked what I wanted to be when I grew up. I said, "I am going to own a number of companies." And now I do, and it's fun. I think it's fun to talk about business. All of my friends own their own companies. My husband owns his own mathematical research and engineering company. Even my friends who are women own their own companies. And to have so many female entrepreneur friends is amazing. It's like a lifeline sent from above. Many of my male friends own their own companies as well. They own law firms, medical practices, construction companies, among others. My whole world, even my social world, involves business owners, which makes it very energizing and exciting.

Business is about creating, and I see it as art. You create something from nothing, you make a dream come true, you make a process happen, you make a building happen, or you provide a service. The cleaning team that cleans our home is fantastic. I'm friends with the owner, and I tell her all the time, "You make our lives so much better." So as a business owner, you have the opportunity to make people's dreams come true, to make their lives easier. The sellers I work with have dreams as well. They have dreams to retire, move to the next level, or finally realize all of the cash value in the business they have created. And I get to help sell it for them. One of the sellers I recently worked with received $5 million for his business and was extremely excited. It was the most money they had ever received in a lump sum. And they were in that business for 42 years – they retired upon the sale of the business.

Getting to be a part of helping people realize their dreams is incredible. I feel lucky that I happened upon a career that I was really good at and started in this career when I was young. After 23 years of plowing the fields and sowing the seeds of the business world, we get a lot of referrals. I feel very, very lucky for that.

■ What should people look for when choosing a business broker? And when should they begin their search?

Jackie Ossin Hirsch: In early 2022, I sold an HVAC business. I first started speaking with the owner in 2014. So it can be a long sales cycle. What I do isn't always fast - but it is correct. Different businesses and business owners need different amounts of time to get the business saleable.

For a business I sold in February of 2022, I first met with them at the beginning of August 2021. They were referred to me, and they said, "We want to put it on the market next week." So sometimes, you get that. And that's what we did. We put it on the market the next week, and we had it under contract by the end of the year. So you get different types.

But if you're thinking about it and don't have an exit strategy, you should meet with a broker. In fact, I think you should meet with a few brokers. And you really need to understand what your business is. Is it local? Is it relocatable? How does the business broker work? Do they package the business properly? One of the main problems I see is that businesses are not packaged properly, and fewer than 10% of businesses that go to market actually sell. Most people don't even know that statistic. It's kind of horrific. In our office, we have a 90% sales rate. But that's because we are very specific about what we take, and we have it packaged well so that a buyer can buy it. You have to understand what your process is, what their process is, and they have to be aligned with your goals. It's going to depend upon where you live too. Many brokers are semi-retired and only do a deal here and there. That's not what we do in our office. We always aim to get top sales and are one of the leading firms in Central Florida. And we always work full time. Somewhat jokingly, I say, "From January to May, we work seven days a week." It's a hectic time of year, and we work extremely hard. That's how we close so many deals and how we break records. So you've got to figure out what you want and look at how hard the broker hustles and go from there.

How can people find you, connect with you, and learn more?

Jackie Ossin Hirsch: You can email me at jackie@crowneatlantic. com. Our office number is 407-478-4101. We primarily work in the South. We're licensed in Florida, but we help people buy and sell companies throughout the United States. We work with online companies all the time, and we have a ton of online buyers. Every company needs to be properly packaged. When somebody lists an online business for sale, a lot of times, it's not packaged correctly, with the result being that it does not sell. At Crowne Atlantic, we make sure the package gets created correctly.

JACKIE OSSIN HIRSCH

Founder/Certified Business Intermediary (CBI)

Crowne Atlantic Business Brokers

Jackie Ossin Hirsch is a licensed business and real estate broker with over two decades of experience. In 2004, she founded Crowne Atlantic Properties, LLC, which focuses on the sale of businesses in the manufacturing, construction, online, large restaurant, service, retail, and technology industries.

Jackie has extensive business sales experience, including transactions involving stock, cash, seller financing, and SBA financing. She has worked on over 400 transactions and specializes in companies with a value of $1MM to $50MM and EBIT from $500,000 to $10MM.

She is a recognized expert in business valuations and has provided over 500 valuations for estate planning, divorce, bankruptcy, partnership buyout, and refinancing. She has also testified as an expert witness in divorce and bankruptcy courtroom proceedings.

Jackie has the distinction of being a Certified Business Intermediary (CBI) with the International Business Brokers Association (IBBA). There are fewer than 1000 CBI's worldwide. The CBI is a prestigious designation awarded to intermediaries who have proven professional excellence through verified education as well as exemplary commitment to the business brokerage industry. Her knowledge and perspective of being in the marketplace enables her to confidentially match the right buyer or investor group with the right business opportunity, ensuring a successful business transaction and business transition.

As a result of her dedication to her clients, Jackie has won numerous business brokerage industry awards from the Business Brokers of Florida (BBF), and has been a Million Dollar producer every year.

She has honorably served for five years on the local Orlando BBF Board, in addition to the Florida BBF Board.

Jackie holds a bachelor's degree from the University of Florida, majoring in Business Administration and minoring in Spanish and Latin American Studies. In addition, Jackie studied International Business at the University of Costa Rica while becoming fluent in Spanish.

As a Central Florida native, Jackie has intimate knowledge of Florida business locations, neighborhoods, infrastructure, and demographics. She has traveled to over 30 countries and is adept at relating to any buyer or seller.

Jackie takes great pride in serving her clients on each side of the table, and one of her greatest joys is seeing her clients succeed.

EMAIL:

jackie@crowneatlantic.com

PHONE:

407-478-4101

WEBSITE:

www.crowneatlantic.com

LINKEDIN:

https://www.linkedin.com/in/jackieossinhirsch/

JASON HULLENDER

CONVERSATION WITH JASON HULLENDER

> ■ **Jason, you are the founder of IAG M&A Advisors in Addison, Texas. Tell us about your work and the people you help.**

Jason Hullender: We specialize in working with the lower middle market segment across the US and Canada. We are one of the few M&A Advisors to work with smaller businesses from half a million up to 50 million in gross revenues. I've been doing mergers and acquisitions and working with clients for almost 30 years now. My father introduced me to the business of doing mergers and acquisitions. After that, I spent a little time in the military, returned, and started running the business development department for another M&A firm in Dallas. Then in 2009, we started IAG M&A Advisors. So we've been working with a couple of hundred clients yearly and have a team of experienced M&A advisors who work with the client hands-on. We take them through the whole process from start to finish.

■ **What questions do you hear from owners thinking about selling their business?**

Jason Hullender: Most times, clients are not prepared to go through the process of selling their business. They have no idea what it takes to get their business sold and what things buyers will look for when they start the process. So we have to educate them on what buyers will look for. We look at their financials, help them understand the add-backs and adjustments in the business, and really help to get them prepared. A valuation is an essential step in the process. Expectations often are not in line with what the owners think the business is worth and what the market says it is actually worth, so we work to bridge that gap. Owners often have questions about who the buyer will be, thinking they might be acquired by a large strategic or private equity firm. Still, that doesn't end up being the buyer for their business in many cases. It depends on synergies and what the buyer is looking for.

■ **What are the costs associated with selling a business?**

Jason Hullender: This is the question we are asked the most. The costs associated with selling your business commonly include costs associated with any optimizations, valuations and percentages of the final selling price paid to the intermediary selling your business.

Other costs may include paying for any outside services you choose to hire, such as a lawyer or accountant.

■ How long does it take to sell a business?

Jason Hullender: We have a proven process for selling your business. However, there are other time factors to consider when selling. The US Small Business Administration statistics show that it normally takes six months to one year to sell a business after being listed. However, the timeline can vary due to factors such as buyer diligence, market conditions, and how optimized your business is to sell.

■ Are there myths and misconceptions about selling a business?

Jason Hullender: Sellers often get advice from the internet, their peers, and some use online valuation tools. Perhaps they hear about someone who sold their business for multiples of revenue or a much higher multiple of EBITDA than the norm. But typically, we find that businesses won't sell for multiples of revenue and will fall within a normal range based on their industry. So that's a misnomer. It will usually be a multiple of the EBITDA or the free cash flow of the business called SDE, which is the seller's discretionary earnings. So that's one thing we sometimes have to explain and educate owners about.

Another misconception involves transition periods. Sometimes sellers think they can just hand over the keys to the buyer and be out of the business in a few months. But often, the owner is vital to the business operation and will stick around for six months to a year on average.

■ How has the "Great Resignation" impacted your market?

Jason Hullender: We've seen a significant uptick in buyers leaving corporate America this past year. Even going into this year, we're seeing more and more buyers looking to control their own destiny. They have capital that they've put together, and lending is outstanding. Right now, we're seeing some of the best lending environments that we've ever seen in our history. And then there's a lot of capital on the sidelines from different buying groups compounded by a lot of competition. So it is a great time for an owner to be considering selling the business because of all these external factors that are going on in the marketplace right now.

We're seeing a lot of individuals with capital. Many have already been pre-approved with SBA, and they have lenders ready to go. Many of our deals are happening with these types of buyers.

■ **How far ahead should an owner prepare their business for sale?**

Jason Hullender: You should start preparing your business three to five years before a proper exit. The first thing is to start working on your financials and showing more profit. In M&A, cash is King, and if the financials show the true potential for the business to generate cash flow, the buyer will tend to pay more for the business than one where all the cash is hidden. Then look at your processes and systems and make sure your business is not 100% dependent on you. This is the time to look at "value drivers" and make improvements. Take your business to the market when you know things are on an upper trend. We have something we use called the "Value Builder." John Warrillow created it, and we've been using it a long time. It's a good gauge for the different value drivers in a client's business that we can use to make improvements if they're not ready to go to market right now.

■ **Jason, what inspired you to get started in this field?**

Jason Hullender: I'm passionate about helping sellers achieve the goal of exiting their business. It's very rewarding to help somebody transfer one of the largest assets they'll probably ever have and help them go on to the next chapter of their lives. It is equally rewarding to help buyers acquire businesses. Sometimes we have buyers who come back to us after selling them a business, which becomes an ongoing legacy. But it's just been a passion of mine for many years to get involved in mergers and acquisitions and start learning some of the things that will make me a good deal maker and help clients achieve their goals.

■ Is there anything else you would like to share?

Jason Hullender: Valuation is important. Working with a good M&A advisor or intermediary will help set the right expectations when going into a transaction. We can help take you through the process and work with other advisors in the deal, such as attorneys, accountants, and financial advisors. It's our job to set you up for success.

■ How can people find you, connect with you, and learn more?

Jason Hullender: Our website is www.iagmerger.com. You can also email me directly at jhullender@iagmerger.com. We can set up a time for a discovery call to learn a little more about your business and see if we would be a good fit. We can talk you through the process of how we would go about helping you exit your business.

JASON HULLENDER, "CM&AA", CBB

Managing Director

IAG M&A Advisors

Jason Hullender is a Certified Merger and Acquisition Advisor and IAG M&A Advisors Managing Director. After co-founding IAG in 2009, Jason quickly grew it into one of North America's premier M&A advisory firms. He is passionate about helping other entrepreneurs receive the exit they deserve. His team has assisted hundreds of sellers in valuing and eventually exiting their businesses. Prior to starting IAG, he led the marketing division of another M&A firm and has been serving clients for 20 plus years before and after proudly serving in the United States Marine Corps.

EMAIL:

jhullender@iagmerger.com

PHONE:

972-331-6578

WEBSITE:

www.iagmerger.com

OTHER:

www.buyyourbiz.com

FACEBOOK:

https://www.facebook.com/iagmerger/

LINKEDIN:

https://www.linkedin.com/company/iag-llc

TWITTER:

https://twitter.com/iagmerger/

JOSHUA
CARNES

CONVERSATION WITH JOSHUA CARNES

■ **Joshua, you are the President of Lion Business Brokers in Austin, Texas. Tell us about your work and the people you help.**

Joshua Carnes: Lion Business Brokers was founded to provide a higher level of service that I felt wasn't being offered by lower mid-market advisory firms in the industry. We pride ourselves on delivering that elite level of service that you would generally only get with a larger international brokerage firm but on a much more personal level. As a company, we have three main areas of focus: Business Sales, Mergers & Acquisitions, and Business Advisory.

■ **What is the most common question from business owners wanting to sell?**

Joshua Carnes: One of the first questions we get asked is, "What is my business worth?" We believe it all starts with a number. You either like that number, or you don't. Our job is to provide you with enough information to make an informed decision on if now is the right time to sell, and if not, help you take the necessary steps to do what you need to do to get your business to a number that suits your exit goals and objectives. So for us, and most business owners that we talk to, it all centers around that listing valuation and what their business could sell for on the market today.

■ How has the "Great Resignation" impacted your industry?

Joshua Carnes: It's had a really interesting impact. Two to three weeks post COVID, the buyers already started to hit the market. Pre-COVID, we would get one to two emails from buyers reaching out to us every couple of weeks. And I'm talking about larger firms, private equity, or family money firms. Now it's three to four emails a week, and we are getting phone calls, "Hey, what do you got? Do you have anything on the back burner?" So the buyers have definitely ramped up their interest, and there's a lot more of them. But one of the other things that is happening is the "Great Baby Boomer Exodus." It's been rumored to be coming for several years. We see business owners getting tired; they've been working for 30 plus years, survived the 90s, the 2000s, and everything else economically and personally, and are looking to exit. So the next three to five years will be an exciting time in this industry. If your business was making money during COVID, it would sell for a premium today.

■ Are there myths and misconceptions about selling a business?

Joshua Carnes: One of the most interesting misconceptions I see in this industry is the business brokers being mixed in with commercial real estate brokers or thinking that commercial real estate brokers and business brokers are the same things. We are not; commercial real estate brokers are a great referral source for us. We partner with commercial real estate brokers and refer out all real estate transactions. The reality is the two industries are closely related but are two very separate and distinct industries with two different skill sets. We do absolutely no commercial real estate in our office. We refer that out to the professionals or the attorneys. We recommend sellers start the conversation with an experienced business broker.

■ What is the first thing business owners who are considering selling should do?

Joshua Carnes: Get your financials in order, get your business show ready. Many business owners don't have their financials together or accurately packaged. And this is the first thing that any potential buyer is going to want to see. Packaging your business financials is a substantial piece of the puzzle. Also, just like getting a house ready to sell, you will need to get your business ready to show in all areas. The better the presentation, the better chance you have at getting a premium for your business.

■ Joshua, what inspired you to get started in this field?

Joshua Carnes: My personal start is kind of funny. I had just exited my own business as a marketing consultant and was getting ready to enter the real estate industry. I had a friend who was a business mentor and life coach for me. We sat down, and I showed him my business plan and everything I had planned out. And he said, "So you're really going to drive around with people in the back of your car and put on a smile and show them houses? That's not you." And I said, "What are you talking about? There's a ton of money in that industry. I can do it." And he said, "Hey, why don't you talk to my friend who is a business broker? It's a lot like real estate for businesses." And long story short, we're going on year seven now. It's the best decision I've ever made. I love the industry, love helping business owners, and couldn't be happier.

■ What should people consider when choosing a business broker?

Joshua Carnes: One of the things we recommend that everyone do is talk to multiple brokers. You're about to enter into a year-long relationship with this business broker. A personality aspect will come into play, and you will let this person into every part of your business. So you want to make sure that the business broker is someone you not only trust but someone you actually want to work with over the next year. Because once you hire them, they are all in for the next year trying to get your business sold.

An important question to ask is, "How are you going to market my business?" Take a look at some of their sample marketing material and ask to see a sample CBR (Confidential Business Review). The CBR is an industry-standard marketing package and the primary way your business will be presented to potential buyers. You would be surprised at how archaic the industry is by nature. It's an old industry. Some people just don't take the time to market these businesses properly. Look at sample marketing and make comparisons to find the broker to best represent you and your business.

■ How can people find you, connect with you, and learn more?

Joshua Carnes: Our website is a great place to start www. LionBusinessBrokers.com. We provide free listing valuations to business owners whether they are ready to sell or not. We have agents who represent all of Texas as well as most of the southeast. We're always happy to help anyone out.

JOSHUA CARNES

President, M&A Advisor

Lion Business Brokers

Joshua takes a measured and analytical approach to Mergers and Acquisitions, armed with data and research that helps business owners reach the right audience of potential buyers. As President of the company, Joshua brings clients an impressive background in marketing and consulting, with extensive training from the hands of a former CMO of Oracle. Years of high-level strategic marketing experience helped prepare Joshua to lead Lion Business Brokers and its successful team of Mergers and Acquisition Advisors.

Selling a business takes trust, and Joshua has worked hard to build that over his career. Joshua relies on lessons he learned while working for both privately and publicly held national and international companies to get the job done. "Our goal is to set the bar high on the level of service business owners should expect when engaging with professionals in the M&A industry," he says. Every deal he and his team facilitate requires laser-focused attention to detail.

Joshua looks for advisors like himself, experts who are ready to handle every step of the process, to help business owners make informed decisions. "I love working with business owners," Joshua says. "Every transaction is unique and brings its own set of challenges. I'm a problem-solver. There is no boring repetition in this industry." In addition to attention to detail, confidentiality is key when selling a business, and Joshua works diligently to ensure all transactions remain private.

Selling a business is a life-changing moment for the seller — and the buyer. Joshua considers it an honor to be a trusted advisor in the journey of selling a business. Joshua is less interested in the number of clients Lion Business Brokers brings on, as he provides a superior level of customer service to the clients they have. Lion Business Brokers takes a team approach to everything it does, with staff working together to get the best outcome for clients.

Outside of the office, Joshua's life centers on his three sons. He is actively involved with the local youth sports leagues, and volunteers to coach his sons' football and soccer teams. The U.S. House of Representatives has recognized Joshua for his work with at-risk youth.

Joshua is a member of the International Business Broker Association, a Certified Business Broker by the North American Alliance of Business Brokers, and is recognized as an Industry Expert by Business Brokerage Press Inc. & Business Reference Guide.

EMAIL:
jcarnes@LionBusinessBrokers.com

PHONE:
512-721-8683

WEBSITE:
www.LionBusinessBrokers.com

FACEBOOK:
www.facebook.com/LionBusinessAdvisors

LINKEDIN:
www.linkedin.com/company/lion-business-brokers

ROBERT LATHAM

ROBERT LATHAM

CONVERSATION WITH ROBERT LATHAM

> ■ **Robert, you are the founder of Altapraem M&A Advisors in Texas. Tell us about your work and the people you help.**

Robert Latham: Altapraem is a lower middle market business advisory. We work primarily with people on the sell-side. So we represent owners of businesses who are looking to sell. The industry tends to be sell-side oriented, but occasionally, we help people on the buy-side of the transaction. Often, the company is already in business and wants us to go out and find them another business that they think would be a good fit for them. Our market is Texas and the surrounding states. We work with businesses anywhere from $2 million to $50 million in value, with roughly the same in revenues. Our firm focuses on industrial companies such as manufacturing, distribution, maintenance, logistics, and warehousing. I spent about 20 years in manufacturing and ten years in construction, so my background allows me to understand the business owners I work with and their specific needs. As I like to say, if you make it, move it or maintain it, we probably understand your business well.

■ How informed are business owners about the selling process when they first reach out to you?

Robert Latham: Usually, the larger the business, the more informed. But regardless of size, most of the time, this is the first and only time they are selling a business. It's a big decision to sell and a big decision as to who will help them through this daunting process. They may get information from trusted advisors, such as a CPA and an attorney. Perhaps they have a wealth advisor or a financial planner. So those are the people they tend to rely on. Sometimes advisors give them accurate information, while other times it's wildly off. So a lot of our job in talking to a potential client for the first time is making them aware of the reality of the marketplace.

■ What are the most common questions you hear from sellers?

Robert Latham: "What is my business worth?" and "How much do you charge?" Of course, the answers to those questions vary. But in general, it doesn't vary a lot, and it hasn't varied much over time either.

Several industry groups have done studies, and from the 70s to the current day, the multiples of earnings tend to be very narrow in their range for a given type of business. In determining what a likely multiple is, we look at two different kinds of earnings measures. One is called EBITDA, which stands for earnings before interest, taxes, and depreciation. It's a rule of thumb, and you can undoubtedly get more specific in your analysis, but it gives you a very good idea. Typically, for a business with an EBITA of around $500,000 a year to $1,000,000 and up, the multiple will be somewhere between four and six. I get the quarterly reports and updates on the market. It's a very steady number. As you go up in size to maybe $20 million in revenues, that number will begin to creep up to maybe five or six. If it's a hot or sexy industry in fashion right now, those can be higher into the seven and eight, and sometimes even nine times range. But generally, especially for the kinds of businesses that I specialize in, they're pretty stable and solid. Usually, they are in that four to seven times their earnings range. A multiple of earnings is a simplistic rule of thumb that actually derives from a complex set of equations that look at the current value of expected earnings from the business. Ultimately though, the net result of those equations is the multiple we refer to. There is also a limit to what the buyer can pay and still have cash left over each year after debt service and paying themselves a salary to pay their personal bills. We try to show sellers what that looks like so they understand the value from the buyer's perspective and have realistic expectations about what price they will likely get. Unfortunately, part of our job is frequently telling a seller their baby may not be as pretty as they thought.

As far as what we charge, it varies. The bigger the company, of course, the lower the percentage of the sales price our success fee will be. Small businesses tend to be around 10%, while $30 to $40 million companies might only be 3% or 4%. There's usually a small fee upfront that is credited towards the success fee due at the closing of the sale. The larger the expected sales price, typically the larger that upfront fee becomes.

■ How has the "Great Resignation" impacted your particular market?

Robert Latham: I don't know that it's inspired more sellers. But we definitely have seen increased buyer activity over the past year or so, despite the pandemic and many indicators being off. There are still many people out there who have decided they will take the plunge and go out and buy a business. They might have been laid off, or they might be sick of the corporate life and all the stuff that goes with that. Many people have realized you can run a business from a long distance, work remotely, and only go into a physical location a few times a month. The technology to do this has been around for years, but I think living with the pandemic lockdowns made it more socially acceptable. So I think that's opened the doors for many people who thought they couldn't do that previously. Buying a business in existence is a big head start over trying to start one from scratch. It sounds like a lot of money, but you've got automatic revenue and profits coming in from day one. Yes, financing can be difficult sometimes. But it's just a whole lot easier. For anyone that's ever started a business from scratch, they can tell you; it always ended up costing a lot more money and took a lot more time than they thought to get going and start making money.

■ Robert, what inspired you to get started in this industry?

Robert Latham: Well, like a lot of good things, I stumbled into it. It wasn't the grand plan. I decided to shut down my construction business and get into the brokerage side of things through commercial real estate. I had done some M&A work with a couple of companies that I was involved in previously. Because of my financial background and education, I was very involved in the evaluation and the acquisition process. I met with a guy trying to network and drum up business for my commercial real estate brokerage. He was opening the Houston office for the largest business brokerage franchise in the country and now the world. He learned of my background and said, "Well, you know, I'm just opening this office, and it sounds like you'd be a good fit." So I said, "Okay, fine, I'll give it a try. But I'll keep doing my real estate thing." After about three years, I was making good money in both of them, but I was running out of time in the day. I decided that I had a better advantage and background for selling businesses than selling commercial real estate. So I've been doing that for about eight years. This will be my ninth year, and I just started Altapraem M&A Advisors in January 2022. I am excited to start another new business venture (this will be my third), and we've already got our first client in less than a month. So we're up and running! And I do love what I do for a living. I'm an entrepreneur myself, and this job lets me use such a wide spectrum of knowledge and experience that I've gained over the course of my career. Plus, I love helping other entrepreneurs reap the rewards of all their hard work and sacrifice over the years.

■ Is there anything else you would like to share?

Robert Latham: If you are not already experienced in buying or selling a business, the first step is to talk to a business intermediary to get some idea of the process. I speak to buyers all the time, and we are not trying to make money off them. We just want them to be educated to become better buyers.

The other thing I would say is to assemble a good team before you go out into the marketplace. Find an excellent transactional CPA and a transactional attorney. Don't hire a guy who's writing wills and making business contracts or handling your house purchase. Find someone who's focused on the transaction of a business process. They're much better advisors, and it makes a huge difference. Build that advisory team before taking the next step.

Finally, don't go through this process alone if you're a seller. If you choose not to use Altapraem, use somebody. The firm is important; look for depth and system. But the individual you'll be working with, the deal maker, is most important. Look for business experience, industry certifications, a track record of closing deals, and someone you like working with. This process can take well over a year from start to finish. You need to be able to work well together.

■ **How can people find you, connect with you, and learn more?**

Robert Latham: Our website is www.Altapraem.com. That is a word we created from the Latin words Alta and Praemium, which together mean "high reward." When a seller works with us, we will give them the high reward they have worked so hard to achieve in their business. Look up our website, email us, or be old-fashioned and make a phone call. We'd love to talk to you. And even though technology makes travel seem outdated, we still love to work with our clients face to face.

ROBERT LATHAM, BSCE, MBA, CBI, M&AMI

Founder/President

Altapraem M&A Advisors

Robert Latham is the founder and President of Altapraem M&A Advisors. Prior to forming Altapraem, he was the Vice President and a top producing broker of the Houston office of Transworld Business

Advisors, closing more deals than any other agent. Joining them in the first year of operations, he was a key contributor to their rapid growth over the next eight years. With over 30 years of hands-on managerial experience and a uniquely broad range of skills, experiences, and abilities, Bob has a rare perspective when working with clients to achieve their business objectives. His key attributes in deal-making are creative problem solving, attention to detail, and follow-through.

Bob has worked in a wide spectrum of industries, including heavy manufacturing, petrochemical equipment, aerospace and defense, construction, gas transmission, plastics, and commercial real estate brokerage and investment. Positions held include Owner/Founder of a light construction company, President and COO of ATG Group, a plastics manufacturer, and VP of Business Development and Director of Operations for a petrochemical equipment manufacturer (ultimately acquired by Oceaneering). Bob has a BS in Civil Engineering from Texas A&M University and an MBA from Columbia University Business School in New York City. Demonstrating his commitment to excellence in his chosen profession, he is an active member of the International Business Brokers Association and The M&A Source. He has also achieved the industry designations of Certified Business Intermediary and the more demanding M&A Master Intermediary. His interests include automobile restoration, cooking, and flying, including being a volunteer pilot for Angel Flight, and he once sailed across the Atlantic.

EMAIL:

Bob@Altapraem.com

PHONE:

713-463-9222

WEBSITE:

www.Altapraem.com

BEN
HARGIS

BEN HARGIS

CONVERSATION WITH BEN HARGIS

> ■ **Ben, you are the owner of Mach 10 Enterprises and a business broker with California Business Brokers in Southern California. Tell us about your work and the people you help.**

Ben Hargis: I help find buyers and sellers and put the two together for the business brokerage aspect. As a business intermediary, I help facilitate the deal. I ensure that owners have an advocate on their side and help buyers make purchases that are right for them. I work with all different types of businesses. On occasion, I will bring in experts to help with the specifics of a deal, depending on the industry. Sometimes industry-specific businesses have nuances that may require an additional set of eyes. The most significant aspect of facilitating a deal is that the business being sold makes money. If the business is making money and has good cash flow, it's a win-win for the buyer and the seller.

When it comes to who I am willing to help, the short answer is anyone. Most people don't know where to begin when it comes to selling or buying a business. Sellers often think that their business is worth significantly more than the market values it for, and buyers do not know what they should be looking into when determining what's right for them. When someone is so engulfed in their industry, bringing me in as a business broker can shed some light on how their industry is evolving, which may change the perspective of those rose-colored glasses.

I'm happy to consult with anyone on either side of the table to see what they are looking for, what their goals are, and then what the best fit may be. People can easily get lost in this process, so it's necessary to have an expert like myself on their team to be their guide.

■ How informed are sellers when they first reach out to you?

Ben Hargis: I would say 90% of sellers need a lot of help structuring the deal. Maybe they thought about handing off the business to their kids, but their kids decided they didn't want to be in that industry. Many business owners believe their business is worth a certain amount. When they try to sell it without a broker, they quickly find out the harsh reality that it's not anywhere near the dollar amount they had envisioned. Sellers then look to me as their professional to get a realistic valuation of their company or business and finally begin to understand and feel the value of my services. Their time as an owner is valuable. Sellers often still have the day-to-day business to run, and taking on my role is not feasible. My skill set in finding a buyer requires wearing a different hat.

■ Are there myths and misconceptions about selling a business?

Ben Hargis: There are a lot of misconceptions out there. It's not like a house; you can't put a "For Sale" sign on the front door and let everybody come by and take a look at it. There are no open houses. That's not how it works. There are a lot of confidentiality agreements. You can't blast it out there to everybody and have buyers coming out of the woodwork. You don't want the secret sauce of why your business makes so much money to leak out. It's not for everyone to know. The business owner who buys it wants to keep that secret sauce to themselves as a proprietary asset. The steps you have taken to get your business to where it is should be a confidential matter. The owner doesn't want their vendors, clients, or employees to know the business is being handed off to another owner. The employees might get cold feet and start looking for other job opportunities when they hear a new owner is stepping in. So it might be a great step; it might be a horrible step. But either way, you want to keep it under wraps until the deal is solidified. Then you can share it with everybody on a "need to know" basis.

■ **Why do owners typically have inflated ideas about the value of their business?**

Ben Hargis: I think part of it is emotion. Most owners feel that they have worked so hard that their business should be worth, let's call it, a million dollars. In reality, it comes down to the balance sheet, the financials, and having a CPA or business valuation expert to value the business. It is not based on emotion or the potential of the business. Some sellers will say to the new buyer, "Well, you could do X, Y, and Z, and then this business will be worth $5 million." The new buyer usually would say, "If it's such a great deal, why didn't you take advantage of that? Why didn't you jump through those hoops to make your business more valuable?" Sellers can over glorify the potential of their business and what "could be." Sometimes the amount of work involved in the potential can be overwhelming to a buyer who can quickly get cold feet. Emotion is undoubtedly one of the most significant contributors to inflated ideas about value, so it's critical that you have me as your broker handling those conversations and realistically navigating the details.

■ **How has the "Great Resignation" impacted your market?**

Ben Hargis: There are different levels to what is going on. We have the baby boomer generation nearing retirement age, not only in Southern California but across the rest of the country. Many people have worked really hard in the past several years; the economy has been good. Home prices have inflated to give people that sense of comfort and wealth. It makes people feel like it is a great time to be selling their businesses. Things have gone well, prices are high, and they are ready to give up the long hours they put in during the last 10 to 12 years of good economic times. People are ready to go off into the sunset and enjoy life a little bit.

Service businesses are usually great businesses when retirees want to retire. They are generally good money generating businesses in good times and tough economic times. As an extra interesting bit of insight, in this post-Covid world, we're seeing an upswing of eCommerce businesses going for sale geared toward those who want to work from home. Also, as the Ukraine Russian situation escalated in 2021, cyber security businesses have become the place to be. Lots of interest in how to protect customers' data and the multiples these companies are fetching is really intriguing.

■ Ben, what inspired you to get started in this field?

Ben Hargis: I like real estate a lot, but I feel like so many people are in that space. I just wanted to differentiate myself. I like business. I enjoy helping people. I'm an entrepreneurial spirit at heart, and working with businesses just fits for me. I appreciate people that have taken risks and been rewarded. I understand where they come from; it's a tough thing to start a business, run it, do it well, and then exit with the most money in their pocket to enjoy the fruits of their labor. For me, it just seemed like business brokerage was a much more pleasing, rewarding career.

■ Is there anything else you would like to share?

Ben Hargis: The cost of money right now is phenomenally advantageous to purchasing a business. If you go out and start a business from scratch, it takes years and years to build it up and get that cash flow going. But if you buy a business using low-interest rate money, the banks are just flushed with cash right now. And I don't think a whole lot of people are taking advantage of low-interest rates and inflation. It just benefits you to borrow the money now because, in the future, the value of the money will be less. I don't think many people are taking advantage of the easy money right now. Also, whether it is good economic times or bad economic times, you need a broker to help make these transactions run smoothly.

■ How can people find you, connect with you, and learn more?

Ben Hargis: I wear many hats. I'm the host of Mach 10 Radio on Youtube. I am also the Executive VP of Flight Ops at EBA Jets, currently raising 20 million dollars to create a fractional ownership model to surpass the success of NetJets. As a motorcycle enthusiast, I usually find solutions to challenges when I'm on the open road. I meditate daily and find that easy and peaceful things usually work out. With strong effort and struggle, they rarely do. If you want to buy or sell a jet, I can help you out. If you want to buy or sell a home, I can help you out. If you want to find businesses or commercial property to invest in, I can help you out. If you have a business that you would like me to consult on or do PR for, I can help you out. You can reach me at ben@mach10enterprises.com.

If you are ready to buy or sell a business, you can reach me at ben@californiabusinessbrokers.com. Even though we are based in California, I am not limited geographically to the state. My North American reach and network run nationwide as well as Mexico and Canada, email me, let's do a deal.

BEN HARGIS

Airline Captain, Entrepreneur, Business Broker, Real Estate Agent

Mach 10 Enterprises

Ben is an entrepreneur through and through. As a result, that puts him in a unique position to understand a business, what makes it tick, and how to navigate the process of moving it from one owner to another. With an affinity for helping people, Ben aims to fuel any

client's success with an abundance mindset. He lifts you up, encourages you to aim high, inspires you, and cheers you on toward fun and exciting endeavors. This is also the main staple in his Mach 10 Enterprises mission statement. It is this personal creed that separates Ben from other Business Brokers or other professionals in his various arenas and has him ready and willing to help anyone in any field or connect people into his personal network.

Ben is also a veteran airline pilot with more than 20,000 hours under his belt. Exploring the world on foot or on motorcycle, Ben has enjoyed visiting countries worldwide. He feels at home in the water and appreciates the peace that comes with meditation. He is also an incredibly proud father to two boys and a new grandpa bringing a new level of joy to his life.

EMAIL:
ben@mach10enterprises.com

WEBSITE:
www.mach10enterprises.com

KATE
VRINER

KATE VRINER

CONVERSATION WITH KATE VRINER

■ **Kate, you are the Vice President of Sunbelt Business Advisors of Southwest Ohio. Tell us about your work and the people you help.**

Kate Vriner: I work with business owners in all areas, with up to $2 million in EBITDA (earnings before interest, tax, depreciation, and amortization). We sell everything from manufacturing facilities, trucking companies, home health care, convenience store drive-thrus, and restaurants. We focus on businesses in Southwest Ohio and Northern Kentucky.

■ **What is the number one challenge owners have when selling their businesses?**

Kate Vriner: The number one challenge right now is the workforce. Every industry is having trouble finding employees. Owners are also concerned about what will happen to current employees once they sell the business or how they will react when they find out. So most of the primary concerns revolve around the workforce.

We do our best to keep the transition confidential. When a buyer is coming in, they are buying the cash flow. It can differ depending on the type of buyer you have, but generally, when an individual buys your business, they want your employees and will take great care of them. Without those employees, they won't have the cash flow to run the business and support the customers. Regarding the workforce shortage, we talk to owners about how they can differentiate themselves from their competition and bring on the best people possible.

■ How knowledgeable are owners about selling a business?

Kate Vriner: Most are first-time sellers, but we have some clients with multiple businesses who utilize our expertise when selling an additional business. But in most cases, this is their first and only time selling a business. So we're with them from the beginning to the end of the process, and we help them at each step. We begin by offering a broker's opinion of value to give them a sense of what the market can bear and what buyers will be willing to pay. We take the work off the owner by screening each buyer and prepping them for meetings. Owners often aren't sure what they should be highlighting in the buyer/seller meetings. We tell all of our clients to give us the good, the bad, and the ugly about their business because we need to disclose all of that to the buyers, but in a way that won't scare them off. Often when sellers had an issue in the past that has since been resolved, they aren't sure how to disclose that scenario to a potential buyer.

■ What mistakes do you help sellers avoid?

Kate Vriner: Financials are often an issue. Business owners tend to run their business and handle their finances in a way that works great for them, but it may not be what buyers are looking for from an outside perspective. If an owner is running personal expenses through the business and it is not clear whether they are actually personal, the buyer may not believe it, and the bank may not buy it. Our ideal situation is getting in front of the potential client two to five years before they want to sell to educate them on the importance of getting their books cleaned up. They might have to pay more taxes for a couple of years. In the long run, the return on the sale of their business will make the adjustment worthwhile.

The other big thing is making sure processes and procedures are documented. The seller may know how the business runs, but when they leave, all of that knowledge needs to be in one place for the next owner. Documentation can take a long time, so owners should be working on that right away. It's a living document, so they can make changes as they go. Cross-training employees on the team is hugely beneficial to an incoming buyer in spreading knowledge throughout the company.

- ## Kate, what inspired you to get started in this field?

Kate Vriner: It is a family business. My dad started 16 years ago, and I was on maternity leave with my second child when he talked to me about joining the business. I've been with him for six years now, and we've got a great team. We have a couple of other family members working with us and some non-family members. Before joining the family business, I was in transportation and logistics for a long time. I was the intermediary for our customers, trying to find trucks to ship their freight. My passion is helping people exit as successfully as they can. I love the people who come to us and say they're ready. But I also really love working with people way ahead of time to help make sure that they're ready to go.

- ## Is there anything else you would like to share?

Kate Vriner: It's a great time to sell right now. 2020 was rough on a lot of people. But we've definitely seen an uptick in activity on both the buyer and seller sides. It's a perfect time to at least be exploring the possibility of selling and the options regarding what that sale could look like. Still, especially with the size of the businesses we work with, there are various options for potential buyers. It's important to always keep an open mind about the best fit for your particular business.

■ **How can people find you, connect
with you, and learn more?**

Kate Vriner: Our website is www.sunbeltnetwork.com/dayton-oh/.
An easier way to reach me is by phone at 937-903-7554. You can also
email me at kvriner@sunbeltnetwork.com.

KATE VRINER, CBI, CEPA

Vice President

Sunbelt Business Advisors of Southwest Ohio

Kate Vriner received her BA in Organizational Leadership from Wright State University. Since she began her career as a business intermediary, she received her business intermediary certification (CBI) from the International Business Brokers Association and an exit planning advisors certification (CEPA) from the Exit Planning Institute.

Kate is passionate about assisting business owners in planning and executing their transition from their business. She is currently the Vice President and Senior Broker at Sunbelt Business Advisors of Southwest Ohio and has been with the organization for six years. While her primary focus has been on assisting business owners with finding the right buyers for their businesses, she has started to focus more on assisting business owners in preparing themselves and their businesses for this transition. Kate has found that making sure the business owners are preparing their businesses for the sale and preparing themselves is critical for the success of the sale and life after.

Additionally, Kate is the President of Everybody Plays, a non-profit whose mission is to eliminate inequity in sports in the Greater Dayton Area.

EMAIL:
kvriner@sunbeltnetwork.com

PHONE:
937-903-7554

WEBSITE:
www.sunbeltnetwork.com/dayton-oh

LINKEDIN:
Kate Vriner, CBI

GERRY
CHADWICK

GERRY CHADWICK

CONVERSATION WITH GERRY CHADWICK

■ **Gerry, you are the founder of Sunbelt Business Advisors of Southwest Ohio, serving the region of Dayton/Cincinnati, Ohio, and Northern Kentucky. Tell us about your work and the people you help.**

Gerry Chadwick: We are a full-service business brokerage and low-middle-market M&A firm. We work with clients to understand the sale process and work with them from initial planning to close. These steps include working with the owner to determine the value of their business, identifying areas that may improve value, and making sure there's a good match between the seller's financial goals for selling the business and the actual value of the business. Once we agree on the value, we're then able to market the business confidentially and walk prospective buyers through the steps of buying the business, ultimately leading to the successful transfer of ownership.

We follow a 10-step process:

- Plan and prepare by doing pre-sale due diligence (have the information a buyer will need at the outset and build a narrative around any issues and opportunities with the business).
- Gain agreement on seller objectives and have realistic expectations for the outcome.
- Prepare a valuation.
- Prepare business profile and marketing materials.
- Market the business for sale to a defined target audience and our extensive prospect list.
- Identify and screen buyers - including an NDA.
- Drive towards a contingent offer or terms sheet.
- Assist with the due diligence process.
- Work with both parties to have attorneys prepare closing documents.
- Close - help plan the announcement to employees and customers and build a transition plan.

We are generalists and don't limit our engagements to certain business categories. We've worked on everything from manufacturing shops to salvage yards and IT services to trucking firms. One of the key attributes we seek in our brokers is curiosity. This generates real interest in how a business works, which allows us to ask the right questions in order to understand the key attributes of the business for potential buyers. This sincere interest helps in gaining the trust of the business owner.

Ultimately, our goal is to sell the business at the highest value possible to the right buyer and have both parties smiling at the close of the transaction - and a year later!

■ How has the "Great Resignation" impacted your market?

Gerry Chadwick: Business owners are having a great challenge right now with being adequately staffed. That dramatically impacts their revenues and profits, their value to the market, and how the market looks at that particular business. Everybody is looking for a fully staffed, raring-to-go business. The other side of that is that it's a very active market. We're seeing a lot of new buyers coming in who were put on the bench during COVID, which allowed them to reevaluate their professional careers and say, "I'm not so sure I want to keep doing this. So what else can I do? How can I work for myself?" Buying an existing, cash-flowing business is one of those opportunities.

■ What concerns do sellers have when they first reach out to you?

Gerry Chadwick: There are usually several concerns. If the sale is a step to retirement, some owners are worried about what they'll do with themselves if they sell the business. We've held seminars to address this challenge.

They're undoubtedly concerned about value. In this environment, many businesses saw a dip during 2020 and started to build back up in 2021, but might not be where they were in 2019. So they wonder if they can still get the value for their business that they had a few years ago. One strategy we use is to keep track of trailing twelve-month financial statements to make sure we track the upward trends of the business and can convey the improvements to buyers and lenders.

Owners are concerned about how the process will work and what their responsibilities are to the process. Our goal is to manage the majority of the process to make sure the owner can focus on keeping the business running smoothly.

Occasionally, there can be a misconception that they have to take an offer if somebody gives them an offer. So they're concerned about selling to somebody they don't really want to sell to and who will not continue the culture they built or take care of their employees or customers in the same way. But those are concerns that can be mitigated. Part of our job is to introduce buyers who are the best possible fit for the seller, hopefully leading to an offer and a close.

Finally, and maybe most importantly, they want to ensure no one finds out the business is for sale. When we review how we go to market and the steps we take to maintain confidentiality, this concern is mitigated.

■ Are there myths and misconceptions about selling a business?

Gerry Chadwick: The classic one is the country club urban legend of people thinking they will sell their business for eight to ten times earnings. It's really hard for them to get over that. So we do some modeling that shows them that their adjusted earnings just can't handle a multiple beyond the norm, typically 2.5 to 4 times. So they've already projected what they are going to retire on based upon what Joe said down at the club. And we've got to adjust their mindset for reality.

Business values vary greatly depending on several factors. These include:

- Earnings track record
- Opportunities for growth
- Sustainability of revenues and earnings
- Comparison to competition
- SWOT analysis
- Customer concentration issues
- Ease of operation - are processes and procedures memorialized?
- Management - are there secondary levels of supervisors and managers to assist the owner?
- Employees - are all positions filled, level of expertise to replace them, length of tenure?
- Transferability

The gold standard is conceptually being able to close on Friday, flip the keys to the buyer, and have the buyer ready to go on Monday. Owners who take the time to focus on these areas prior to putting the business on the market will benefit from greater value and marketability of the business.

■ What common mistakes do sellers make?

Gerry Chadwick: The biggest mistake is not adequately preparing. We do webinars and seminars and send out information via email and newsletters to encourage business owners to start the planning process now. It doesn't matter if you're one, three, or five years away; start the planning now by allowing us to do a business valuation to see where you are. I use the GPS analogy, "You can't figure out where you're going if you don't know where you're starting from." People are resistant to doing that. We hear from accountants and attorneys that they're preaching the same thing to their clients. And they're still reluctant to get the planning process started.

Secondly, when you are trying to find the answers to questions regarding the sales process, call a firm like Sunbelt or another professional business brokerage firm that will provide a fact-based recommendation. Unfortunately, there are plenty of people who are willing to give advice. In general, an owner shouldn't listen to them. The other day, we talked to a seller whose friend said, "Don't replace the unfilled positions with new employees because the buyer will come in with their own team." This couldn't be more incorrect. As hard as it is to find employees right now, an owner needs to be as fully staffed as possible. So if a buyer comes in and they've got some additional team members, all the better.

Filling positions is one of the most critical jobs of an owner and one of the most important value drivers of the business. I had an owner who lost three critical employees and left over a million dollars of value on the table by not taking the time to replace them.

■ Gerry, what inspired you to get started in this field?

Gerry Chadwick: Well, it's almost embarrassing. I was VP of sales for a company headquartered here in Dayton, and I wasn't always in agreement with the company's direction. That went on for a while. So I started to look around for what I could do outside of this company. That was in 2005, and in Dayton, there weren't many opportunities for me to get the same compensation and responsibilities. So I thought, "If I'm so smart, I should put my money where my mouth is and start my own business." I looked around at many things, and back then, there weren't search engines for "businesses for sale," so I was primarily talking to franchisors of B2C businesses in the foodservice industry, which wasn't for me. Then I came upon Sunbelt, which happens to be a franchise. It was B2B, primarily a sales and marketing function with some technical and financial components. Although it had been a while, I figured I could dust off or relearn the accounting and financial aspects of the job. The bottom line was that I was comfortable doing this kind of work - calling on C-level leaders became business owners, working on multimillion-dollar projects became selling multi-million dollar businesses. It looked like it was a sweet spot for me. It's turned out to be everything I hoped it would be.

■ What should people look for when choosing a business broker?

Gerry Chadwick: Make sure they establish a dialogue and generate a sense of trust. The business is your baby. It's your life's work. Make sure you know the person that you're dealing with. They should be honest and able to provide you with the consultative value that is part and parcel of their responsibilities. Indeed, ask for references from businesses the broker has sold in the past. During the conversations, ask yourself, "Does it sound like this person has done it before? Do they know what they are talking about? Are they listening to me and responding with ideas and suggestions that make sense?"

■ How can people find you, connect with you, and learn more?

Gerry Chadwick: You can call me at 937-260-8969 or go to info@ sunbeltnetwork.com. Our websites are www.sunbeltnetwork.com/ dayton-oh and www.sunbeltnetwork.com/cincinnati-oh. There is quite a bit of information on our website for a business owner to get a sense of how we work. You can also see our listings and the type of businesses we represent. You can also hit the "Contact Us" button on the website and reach out that way.

GERRY CHADWICK, CBI

Owner/Certified Business Intermediary

Sunbelt Business Advisors of Southwest Ohio

Gerry Chadwick is a specialist in M&A transactions. This includes consulting with clients to make sure the business is "buyer ready," a process that includes financial analysis, business valuations, conducting readiness assessments and value gap analysis. When ready, the Sunbelt team markets the business for sale, screens potential buyers, and drives the process through the offer, negotiation, and close.

In a 30-year sales career, including the role of VP of Sales for Excellence In Motivation, the focus was on question-based and need satisfaction selling. The core of these sales methods was curiosity about a client's business and personal goals. These characteristics are keys to successful M&A and business brokerage transactions. Understanding the critical business characteristics and value drivers of a business through in-depth interviews, translating that knowledge to prospective buyers while keeping each party's end goals at the forefront of negotiation has been the key to his success.

Mr. Chadwick earned his BS in Marketing from the University of Dayton in 1977. In 2008 he received the Certified Business Intermediary designation from the International Business Brokers Association (IBBA).

Mr. Chadwick is a member of IBBA, M&A Source, Dayton Region Manufacturers Association (DRMA), Dayton Rotary Club, and co-founder of The Tour de Gem charity cycling event supporting non-profits in the Dayton region.

EMAIL:

gerry.chadwick@sunbeltnetwork.com

PHONE:

937-260-8969

WEBSITE:

www.sunbeltnetwork.com/dayton-oh; www.sunbeltnetwork.com/cincinnati-oh

FACEBOOK:

https://www.facebook.com/SunbeltBusinessAdvisors

LINKEDIN:

https://www.linkedin.com/company/sunbelt-business-advisors-of-southwest-ohio/

ED
SADLER

CONVERSATION WITH ED SADLER

> ■ **Ed, you are a business broker and owner of Sunbelt Business Brokers of Colorado. Tell us about your work and the people you help.**

Ed Sadler: Sunbelt Business Brokers is the single biggest franchise in the country and the world in the business brokerage sector. We're in Colorado, and we've been here four years. We work with owners who are contemplating selling their business, and we start by helping them determine what it would likely sell for. If they agree to list with us, we go to the market to find the right buyer. While most of our sellers are Colorado-based, the buyers may come from anywhere in the world.

■ How prepared and informed are owners who are thinking about selling?

Ed Sadler: In most situations, owners are selling for the first time. There are some serial entrepreneurs out there who have bought and sold many businesses, but most of the people we're talking to are first-time sellers who have been running their businesses for years. It's been their pride and joy (and primary source of income), but they've decided it's time to sell and move on.

Many times they'll at least think about trying to sell it on their own, but the success rate is pretty low. Instead, we highly recommend using an intermediary, such as Sunbelt to help sell your business. As professional business brokers, we're experts in selling businesses. We don't need to be an expert in the seller's industry, and the owner certainly doesn't need to be an expert in selling a business if they hire an intermediary. Once we explain this, most owners appreciate what we're saying, and that's when they agree to work with us.

■ What makes owners unsuccessful when trying to sell on their own?

Ed Sadler: It can break down anywhere along the sales process. Not listing the business in the right places is usually the first mistake. Most small company buyers come to us through the internet. There are some excellent websites out there, including Sunbelt's, where buyers can search for the type and size of business they want in their desired location. But, sellers may not even know where to list. And if they do, and they start receiving buyer inquiries, they may not know what to do next. At a minimum, they must vet the buyers and, amongst other things, make sure they have the financial capability to buy.

Then there is the due diligence phase, and sellers may not be familiar with the type of data and information buyers will demand to make an informed decision on whether or not to buy the company. A seller's inability to manage the process confidentially and professionally can also have serious consequences.

So there are quite a few ways in which it can fall apart when an owner tries to sell their own company instead of using a business broker.

■ How has the "Great Resignation" impacted your market?

Ed Sadler: There are a couple of different things happening. Despite COVID, the overall economy has been pretty strong the last couple of years, and many asset classes have continued to do well. So on a macro basis, many business owners have experienced opportunities to sell in a good market.

And it's no secret that many sellers are baby boomers thinking about retirement and are now motivated to sell. The complimentary corollary to this is the "Great Resignation," which provides another source of well-qualified buyers looking to do their own thing.

No doubt, the "Great Resignation" has been favorable for owners and sellers of small businesses.

■ What common mistakes do you help sellers avoid?

Ed Sadler: We've had several owners approach us recently who were thinking of selling their businesses for one reason or another. As we start to analyze their information, we realize they're not ready to sell. Some of it is just common sense; the business needs to be profitable and the books in order. While some buyers are interested in turnaround situations, it's fair to assume most small business buyers are seeking profitable companies with reasonable growth opportunities.

We're experts at identifying the maximum value a business owner should be able to obtain when they sell their company. But, to be honest, we can't just make it up if the value isn't there. Some owners will then insist on listing their company for sale with an unattainable and unrealistic asking price to "see what happens." Most prospective buyers will see through this, and both seller and broker risk credibility.

In the small business world, it's also common for individuals to put a variety of expenses through the books that may not be directly related to the business being sold to reduce their tax bill. That's all fine and well, but the seller needs to be prepared to explain it and have it documented, so buyers can better understand and assess the real value of the business they're looking at.

Make sure you're taking care of the basics. The business needs to be profitable, the books must be clean, and the physical space should be neat, tidy, and organized (freshly painted walls can go a long way!) When buyers enter your premises, they'll notice.

Make sure you're taking care of both the big picture and the little things when putting your business up for sale. An owner should expect a buyer to be skeptical and ask probing questions, and a seller needs to be fully prepared for that.

■ What is your compensation structure?

Ed Sadler: We almost always represent the seller and work on a success fee/commission basis only. We don't charge a seller for any costs we incur in preparing to sell the business. Instead, we collect our fee from the proceeds credited to the seller only when the sale transaction closes and buyer funds are exchanged for ownership of the business. With this success-fee structure, we're as motivated as the seller and buyer to get a deal done since we don't get paid otherwise.

The fee will vary for each transaction, and a key determinant is the overall size of the deal.

■ Ed, what inspired you to get started in this field?

Ed Sadler: I'm a charter member of the "Great Resignation!" I had a 35-year career in international banking, pretty much all of it overseas. For the last 11 years, I worked in this space for a major British bank, managing acquisition, divestiture, and closure projects. While I was eager to leave the big corporate world, I was also keen on using the experience and skills I had developed there, and it's been a great transition into business brokering. Obviously, they're two different markets, but the skills and experience gained in the former are 100% relevant to the latter.

■ Is there anything else you would like to share?

Ed Sadler: The first thing you need to know about any asset you own, including your business, is its worth. If you plan to sell your business, we can help you with that. Some business brokers provide the service for a fee, while some do it as part of a package of putting a company up for sale, which is what we like to do. But the first thing you need to do, once you start thinking about selling your business, is find out what it's worth.

Sometimes knowing the probable selling price of the business will be the final incentive for an owner to sell. Other times, we'll point out that a business may not achieve its maximum potential value if it's sold right now. We'll likely give you some pointers on things to consider, or we can even refer you to professional consultants.

Of course, we're always excited to work with business owners who are, in every sense, ready to sell right now. But, just as importantly, we also very much embrace the idea of speaking to owners who are perhaps two to three years away from making that decision; we want to be with them the entire journey.

■ **How can people find you, connect with you, and learn more?**

Ed Sadler: Our website is www.sunbeltnetwork.com/greater-denver-co. You can also reach us by phone at 720-753-8000.

ED SADLER

Owner, Licensed Business Broker, Certified
Main Street Business Broker

Sunbelt Business Brokers of Colorado

Are you looking to sell your business? As the owner of two Sunbelt Business Broker franchises on the Colorado Front Range covering Denver, Boulder, Fort Collins, Greeley, Colorado Springs, and

Pueblo, Ed guides and assists owners in selling their small and medium-sized businesses, allowing them to retire or move on to their next venture.

Is owning a business right for you? More than 75% of U.S. executives want to be in control of their own destiny and run their own business. Ed is a charter member of the "Great Resignation" and now helps buyers find that new company.

Originally from New England, Ed graduated from New York University in 1985. He then enjoyed a highly rewarding and (mostly!) exciting 34-year international banking career in the U.S., Asia, Middle East, and Europe. Sixteen years were in the high-net-worth private banking sector. From 2007 to 2019, Ed managed acquisitions, divestitures, business & office closures, transformation, and restructuring initiatives for a major British bank out of Singapore.

Having formed a business partnership in 2021 with experienced Sunbelt of Western Colorado owners and brokers Kevin and Valerie Brooks, Ed has now brought his experience and skills to the exciting market of Colorado Main Street and Middle Market companies, matching up sellers of great companies to the right buyers.

EMAIL:

esadler@sunbeltnetwork.com

PHONE:

720-753-8000

WEBSITE:

www.sunbeltnetwork.com/greater-denver-co

ABOUT THE PUBLISHER

Mark Imperial is a Best-Selling Author, Syndicated Business Columnist, Syndicated Radio Host, and internationally recognized Stage, Screen, and Radio Host of numerous business shows spotlighting leading experts, entrepreneurs, and business celebrities.

His passion is to discover noteworthy business owners, professionals, experts, and leaders who do great work and share their stories and secrets to their success with the world on his syndicated radio program titled "Remarkable Radio."

Mark is also the media marketing strategist and voice for some of the world's most famous brands. You can hear his voice over the airwaves weekly on Chicago radio and worldwide on iHeart Radio.

Mark is a Karate black belt; teaches Muay Thai and Kickboxing; loves Thai food, House Music, and his favorite TV shows are infomercials.

Learn more:

www.MarkImperial.com
www.BooksGrowBusiness.com

Made in the USA
Coppell, TX
28 September 2022